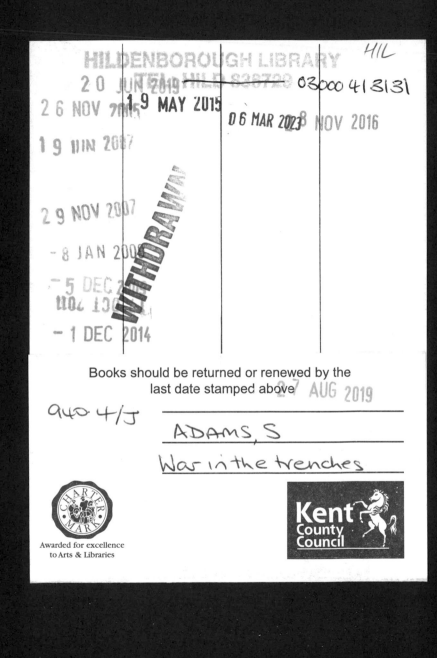

WAR IN THE TRENCHES

WAR IN THE TRENCHES

SIMON ADAMS

FRANKLIN WATTS
LONDON·SYDNEY

Designer Thomas Keenes
Editor Constance Novis
Art Director Jonathan Hair
Editor-in-Chief John C. Miles
Picture Research Diana Morris

© 2004 Franklin Watts

First published in 2004
by Franklin Watts
96 Leonard Street
London
EC2A 4XD

Franklin Watts Australia
45-51 Huntley Street
Alexandria
NSW 2015

ISBN 0 7496 5152 0

A CIP catalogue record for this book
is available from the British Library.

Printed in Malaysia

CONTENTS

THE WESTERN FRONT

In August 1914, war broke out in Europe. The Central Powers of Germany and Austria-Hungary opposed the Allies of Britain, France and Russia. They fought on two main fronts. In the east Germany and Austria-Hungary fought Russia; in the west Germany battled against Britain and France.

TWO FRONTS

In the east the war was very mobile as armies moved back and forth across a wide area. In the west, where the worst fighting occurred, the war soon ground to a halt. Neither side had an advantage. On this front the trenches, which we consider in this book, were dug.

When war broke out, young men across Europe received their call-up papers requiring them to report for military service. Armies were mobilised to full strength and men swapped their civilian lives for a new life in uniform. Britain had no compulsory military service and relied on volunteers to strengthen the army. Everywhere, people were eager to fight for their country, as they believed that victory for their side would be achieved "by Christmas".

HEADING FOR STALEMATE

The German plan was to sweep through Belgium into northern France and swing round to the west of Paris, encircle and defeat the French army in eastern France and then turn their full attention to the far larger Russian army in the east. As the Germans pushed through Belgium towards France, the British army sent a force of almost 100,000 men. At first they too were pushed back at the Battle of Mons, but then the Allies' luck changed. On 2 September, a French military aviator reported that the German First Army to the northeast of Paris had swung south towards the River Marne rather than continue as planned to the west of the city. This change of strategy presented the Allies with an exposed side that could be attacked. The

THE WESTERN FRONT

The Western Front stretched in an S shape from the English Channel south through Belgium and eastern France to the Swiss frontier east of Basle, covering a total of about 760 kilometres. In places it followed natural features, such as rivers, valleys and hilltop ridges, where a series of fortified strongpoints were built, but for most of its length it stretched across flat and open countryside, particularly in northern France and Belgium. It was here that the most important trenches were constructed.

The Allies divided the task of defending their front line between them: the Belgians held the northern 25 kilometres from the coast south to Ypres, the British the 135 kilometres to the Somme and the French the remaining 600 kilometres to Switzerland. When the first US troops arrived in 1918, they took over a 130-kilometre sector north of Verdun from the French.

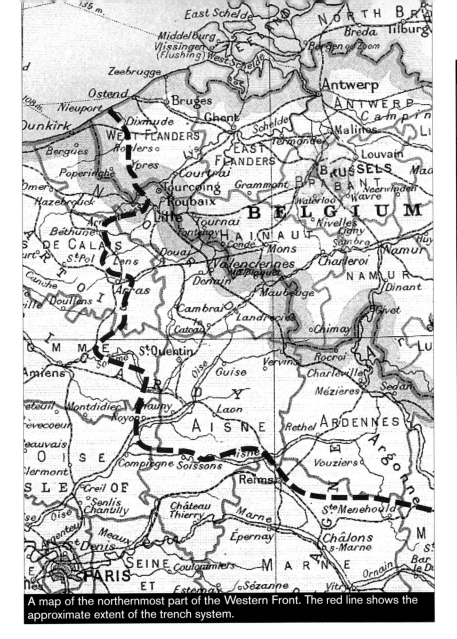

A map of the northernmost part of the Western Front. The red line shows the approximate extent of the trench system.

1914

1 August Germany declares war on Russia; general mobilisation in Germany and France.

2 August German ultimatum to neutral Belgium to allow its troops passage; Germany occupies Luxembourg.

3 August Belgium rejects German ultimatum; Germany declares war on Belgium and France.

4 August German troops enter Belgium; Britain declares war on Germany.

14–23 August Three inconclusive Battles of the Frontiers in eastern France result in stalemate.

20 August Germans take Brussels.

22 August 100,000-strong British Expeditionary Force arrives in France.

23 August–5 September British troops retreat from German advance at the Battle of Mons in Belgium.

5–9 September British and French halt German advance at Battle of the Marne, east of Paris.

15–18 September Inconclusive Battle of the Aisne, northeast of Paris.

18 September–24 November "Race to the Sea" as Allied and German forces try to outflank each other northwards towards the English Channel.

12 October–11 November Inconclusive first Battle of Ypres in Belgium.

German advance was stopped in a battle on the River Marne. They retreated to the River Aisne and dug in.

This caused a deadlock, forcing a change of tactics. South of the river, right down to the Swiss border, both armies had already fought three inconclusive battles and then dug a series of defensive trenches against further attack. The only option was for each army to outflank the other to the north, going round the side to attack from the rear. This so-called "Race to the Sea" continued through the Battle of Ypres until both sides reached the Belgian town of Nieuport in November 1914. As they moved north, both armies built more trenches. By Christmas 1914, two roughly parallel lines of trenches stretched the length of the Western Front.

"... here was a glorious opportunity to break away and look for adventure."

Lieutenant Philip Howe, British soldier, August 1914

THE FIGHTING MEN

By the end of 1914 the Allied armies of Britain, France and Belgium faced the German army along the Western Front. But what size were these armies and who fought in them?

THE BRITISH ARMY

Unlike most other nations, Britain's army was composed of volunteers. As an island, Britain had never faced the same threat of invasion as France or Germany and so had no need to conscript large numbers of men to defend the country. Its army was thus small by continental standards and was in effect a colonial police force keeping the peace in the vast British Empire. Since the Boer War of 1899-1902, when the British had had great difficulty defeating the Boers of South Africa, the British army had been massively reformed. It had a strong high command – the general staff – and had set up an Expeditionary Force within the regular army ready to be sent at speed to Europe should war break out. The various non-regular forces, such as the local militia, were re-organised into a substantial Territorial Force, which trained part-time and could be called into full-time service if it was required.

This army was, however, not nearly large enough for a major European war. In August 1914 it was immediately added to by thousands of volunteers who answered the call of Field-Marshal Lord Kitchener, Secretary for War, to enlist for "king and country". More than 760,000 men volunteered for service in

> ## *"The greatest surge of willing patriotism ever recorded."*

Historian AJP Taylor on Kitchener's Army

A volunteer enlists at a British recruiting station at the start of the war.

KITCHENER'S ARMY

Horatio Herbert Kitchener (1850-1916) was a long-serving soldier who won acclaim for his victories in the Sudan (1896-99) and South Africa (1899-1902). At the outbreak of war, he was appointed Secretary for War in the British government – the first serving officer to hold the post – and immediately issued an appeal for 100,000 volunteers, using his stern face on recruiting posters to urge that "Your Country Needs YOU".

Many of the recruits were organised into local "Pals' battalions", recruited by town mayors or local industrialists. Thus recruits from Newcastle were organised into the Northumberland Fusiliers, while the 3rd Royal Fusiliers was known as the Sports Battalion because it contained two England cricketers and the national lightweight boxing champion. Such local or other connections encouraged recruitment and kept up morale.

"Kitchener's Army" within eight weeks, 33,204 coming forwards on 3 September alone.

THE FRENCH AND BELGIAN ARMIES

The French army was the second largest in Western Europe. Most soldiers were conscripts aged between 18 and 45 serving under the "three years' law" of 1913; the rest were volunteers. To their numbers were quickly added 2,700,000 men conscripted by June 1915. This vast army was designed to match the German army in size and strength, but many soldiers were poorly trained and had little military experience.

As the smallest country, Belgium had by far the smallest army. Because Belgium was neutral, its army did not expect to fight and therefore did not attract high-calibre recruits. It was generally inexperienced and poorly equipped. Compulsory military service was introduced in 1913, enlisting one member from each household.

THE GERMAN ARMY

The German army was by far the strongest and most professional army in Europe as it had long been preparing for war. Its regular army of 700,000 troops could be expanded to almost four million by calling up reservists. Its equipment and training were first rate; its commitment to victory was total.

☞ THE OPPOSING ARMIES IN AUGUST 1914

Britain
- All volunteers, most serving for seven years with five more in the reserves.
- Regular army of 247,432 men, one-third of whom were stationed in India.
- Expeditionary Force of about 100,000 men drawn from the regular army.
- 218,280 reservists and 268,777 Territorials.

France
- Volunteers, plus conscripts serving three years with 11 years in the reserves.
- Regular army of 893,000 men, including 46,000 colonial troops.
- 2,887,000 reservists.

Belgium
- Mixture of conscripts serving up to two years, plus volunteers.
- Regular army of 117,000 troops.

Germany
- Volunteers, plus conscripts: every German man aged 17 to 45 had to serve two years in the army and five in the reserves.
- Regular army of 700,000 troops.
- 3.1 million reservists.

German officer's cap and pre-war military passes. Germany had a large pre-war standing army ready to fight.

DIGGING IN

When soldiers dug the first trenches along the Western Front in autumn 1914, few realised that this would be their home and their security for the next four years. What began as simple defensive ditches soon turned into massive feats of engineering.

TEMPORARY SHELTER

The first trenches were little more than shallow ditches or "scrapes", hastily dug to provide basic cover from enemy fire. Such trenches were only temporary refuges. Generals on both sides believed that "normal" open warfare would resume in the spring. But as time wore on, they became more permanent, and more secure. By 1917, the network of trenches was so extensive that, theoretically, it was possible to walk the entire length of the Western Front without leaving a trench.

NATIONAL DESIGNS

Neither side had great experience at digging trenches, let alone trench warfare, but they quickly, often fatally, learnt from their mistakes. The Germans built trenches where they could best observe and fire at the enemy while remaining concealed. The British and French preferred to gain as much ground as possible before digging in, sometimes perilously close to German lines.

The main difference between the sides was that the Germans dug in on a permanent basis to defend the new ground they had gained in Belgium and France, while the French and British dug in as a temporary measure while they prepared to reclaim territory occupied by Germany. This was reflected in the designs of the trenches. German trenches were elaborate, with deep passageways, wooden walls, shuttered windows and even doormats. The French and British trenches were more makeshift, with few concessions allowed for comfort, although the French often made room for tables with tablecloths on which to eat their meals.

THE TRENCHES

- The Western Front was approximately 760 kilometres long. If both lines of trenches were added together, along with all the frontline, support, reserve and communication trenches, their total length was about 40,000 kilometres. If stretched out, this would have been long enough to encircle the Earth.
- The two front lines faced each other 45 metres to 1.6 kilometres apart across no-man's-land.
- The support trench was 20-90 metres behind the frontline. The reserve trench could be one kilometre or more behind that.
- Access to the whole trench system was from the rear by a lengthy access trench that stretched well beyond the enemy's line of sight.
- Most trenches were at least two metres deep and protected by a bank of earth thrown out during excavation. They measured 60-90 centimetres wide at the base, widening to 1.5 metres at the top of the sloping walls.
- The fire steps along the frontline trench were approximately 60 centimetres high.

British troops in a trench; the periscope allowed safe observation of the enemy.

The basic British trench system consisted of three lines of trenches: frontline, support and reserve. The frontline trench was not straight but sharply angular, designed to limit casualties should a well-aimed shell, or an enemy raiding party armed with a machine-gun, enter the trench. Small lookout trenches ran forwards into no-man's-land to observe the enemy at close range, while fire steps allowed gunners to peer over the edge of the trench in order to take aim at the enemy.

Communication trenches ran from the frontline back to the support trenches. These were where daily life in the trenches was conducted and military orders given. Company headquarters, first-aid posts, cooking shelters, stores of ammunition and other supplies, mortar emplacements and the latrines were all situated off these trenches. Some were underground, while others were open to the skies. Behind these lines was a reserve trench, used as a fallback if the frontline and support trenches were shelled or overrun.

THE CHRISTMAS TRUCE

On Christmas Eve 1914, in the trenches south of Ypres in Belgium, one of the most remarkable events of the war occurred. German troops began to celebrate Christmas with drink and cigarettes, and decorated their trenches with a few candlelit Christmas trees. They then sang a carol: *Stille Nacht, Heilige Nacht (Silent Night, Holy Night)*. The British heard this familiar carol from their trenches opposite and sang *The First Noel*. When they began *O Come All Ye Faithful*, the Germans joined in, singing the same carol in Latin.

On Christmas Day itself, men from both sides met in no-man's-land and exchanged simple gifts. Some played football, using a tin can for a ball if they did not have the real thing, and caps for goalposts, while others posed together for photographs.

The truce spread along perhaps two-thirds of the entire front line, and in some places lasted for a week. No one was punished for failing to fight, but there was no repetition the following Christmas.

TRENCH LIFE

Once the soldiers had arrived at the front and been allocated to their trench, they quickly fell into a daily routine. Fighting was rare. One of the biggest dangers faced by the troops was boredom.

NIGHT AND DAY

Most work in a trench was done under cover of darkness, when the enemy could not see what was going on. This was the time to bring supplies forwards, send out patrols to reconnoitre enemy lines and undertake running repairs to the trenches, frontline parapets and the barbed-wire defensive fences. Stretcher parties went into no-man's-land to rescue the injured and recover the dead. Dawn and dusk were the most likely times of day when the enemy might attack, so troops "stood to" arms, that is, manned the fire steps ready to open fire. At dawn, Allied troops looked out for any German silhouetted against the rising sun. At dusk, the Germans had the advantage.

The days themselves were usually quiet. Those troops not on sentry or other duties took the opportunity to wash and shave, catch up on sleep, keep their rifles in good order, clean and repair their kit, write their diaries or send letters home, read or perhaps paint, draw or play cards. There were no set mealtimes, so soldiers ate as and when they could, sitting in their "funk holes" carved out of the sides of the trench or under waterproof sheets. Officers wrote up their official reports, checked their supplies and prepared for any planned action.

BOREDOM AND FEAR

Daily life in a trench alternated between long periods of sheer tedium, made worse by the discomfort of living partially underground, punctuated by short periods of intense fear when the enemy attacked or bombarded the trench. Such events were rare, however. Far more

MUD AND WATER

The main problem faced by soldiers in the trenches was the wet. Days of rain or snow quickly filled a trench with water, while the network of trenches often interrupted natural drainage systems or broke into underground streams. Although drains were built to take away the water, trenches soon became waterlogged and often collapsed under the pressure of the sodden earth. Waders were issued to many troops, and wooden duckboards were laid on the ground to walk on. Even so the water was often a metre deep.

These damp conditions encouraged rats, which fed on the corpses of soldiers and horses, while body lice were a constant irritant to every soldier. Many soldiers contracted trench fever spread by lice, or "trench foot" – caused by wet feet – which made them red, swollen and painful.

Canadian troops rest in sandbagged trench dug-outs on the Western Front.

☞ **THE KIT**

One British soldier listed the kit he had to carry up to the front line in January 1916:

◆ Two days' rations
◆ Rifle and 150 rounds of ammunition
◆ Great coat and a mack (which he carried)
◆ Pair of mittens and a muffler
◆ One extra pair of socks
◆ Full water bottle, mess tin, mug and cutlery
◆ One blanket rolled in a groundsheet
◆ Pocket primus and a tin of paraffin
◆ A small stove with fuel
◆ Two small tins of baked beans
◆ Three tubes of medicinal vaseline

"I wish you could have seen us," he wrote to his mother. "We looked like animated old clothes shops."

"It has been raining here every day this week which makes things very uncomfortable; heaps of mud and lice including rats of course."

Private AH Hubbard, the Somme, May 1916

common were the intermittent exchanges of gunfire between the opposing trenches. Both sides took every opportunity they could to take pot shots at any enemy soldier foolish enough to show his head above the parapet. Even stretcher-bearers recovering the injured or dead from no-man's-land were likely targets. Raiding parties across enemy lines added to the danger. As a result, sentries were on duty 24 hours a day.

To cope with the stress of trench life, most soldiers spent seven to 10 days at the front before moving back to the reserve lines and then back again, well away from the front itself, to a rest area. Here they could have a bath, clean and delouse their clothes and prepare to return to active duty at the front once again.

WATCHING THE ENEMY

One of the most important aspects of any war is gathering intelligence about the enemy and its intended movements. Information gained is used to mount an attack, or repel an enemy advance. Both sides on the Western Front went to great lengths to gain reliable intelligence.

ON PATROL

Once the trench system was in place by early 1915, it was remarkable how little fighting took place. A number of large, costly battles occurred, but there was often no fighting at all along the entire length of the front for days on end, other than sporadic exchanges of fire between the two trenches. Both sides, however, needed to know what the other intended to do next.

One obvious way was to interrogate enemy prisoners captured in battle or seized by raiding parties at night. The information prisoners revealed, however, was often inaccurate or only partial. It was far better to send out night patrols to probe enemy lines, noting their strengths and weaknesses and where reinforcements and new artillery and other equipment were being stockpiled ready for action. But patrols were a dangerous activity, as they had to cross the rows of barbed-wire fences in no-man's-land, perhaps disturbing unexploded shells. Patrols were always at risk of detection, thus attracting deadly enemy gunfire.

LOOKING OUT

Private Kenneth Garry of the Honourable Artillery Company wrote in his diary in December 1915 what he saw of no-man's-land when he was on guard. "There was nothing to be seen. Only a line of earth and sandbags with the occasional pieces of timber lying about, the whole looking like a mound of earth thrown up by workmen excavating a drain. When you get tired of sitting you can get up and have a peep between the sandbags, and if extra bored you can fire a shot. But a man can be in the trenches a year and need never have a shot, for he would probably not have seen a Hun [a German]."

"We went right up to their [German] barbed wire and located a working party. We could also hear the Huns talking. There was no one however to capture."

Lieutenant Ian Melhuish, writing to his mother on 21 October 1915 about a patrol

German soldiers wade through a sea of mud to rescue an injured comrade from no-man's-land.

LOOKING DOWN

Both sides therefore used observation turrets, sometimes disguised as tree stumps inside which a soldier could climb up some five to seven metres and look down on enemy lines. Frontline soldiers used a periscope – either an official army issue or an improvised one made by attaching a mirror to a rifle or bayonet at a 45 degree angle – to peer above the parapet.

By far the best way to observe the enemy was from the air. Aeroplanes regularly photographed the front lines. The information was used to make detailed maps. Allied commanders were at first suspicious of this newly invented machine – the first-ever flight had only taken place in 1903. However, after the success of a French military pilot in detecting the changed direction of the German army in France in September 1914 (see page 6), aircraft proved their worth above the battlefield. Indeed, their only real threat came from enemy aircraft, leading to some spectacular one-on-one dogfights in the skies above the Western Front.

☛ NO-MAN'S-LAND

The area between the two trenches – no-man's-land – was on average 100 metres to 400 metres wide, although it narrowed in places to 45 metres and widened elsewhere to 1.6 kilometres. It stretched the entire length of the Western Front.

This thin strip was marked out by rows of loosely coiled barbed-wire fences held in place by wooden or metal posts. Shell craters often scarred the ground. The land was devoid of trees and other landmarks because they had all been cleared away to give an uninterrupted view towards enemy lines.

At night, patrols entered no-man's-land to probe enemy lines and observe them at close quarters, but during the day the area was quiet, apart from the sound of birdsong or gunshots.

SUPPLYING THE TRENCHES

Supplying the armies that fought along the Western Front was one of the most crucial aspects of the war. Without food, ammunition and other supplies, the war would have ground to a halt.

CONSTANT DEMAND

The main problem faced by both armies was the sheer length of the front line, and the vast number of soldiers fighting along it. The fighting made it too dangerous to grow, produce or manufacture anything near the line itself. So everything the soldiers required along every kilometre of the line had to be brought up to them on a regular, almost daily basis. Rations to eat, building materials for the trenches, ammunition for guns and

"I packed my trunk, my brown kitbag and two boxes of saddlery."

Walter Bloem, reserve officer in the German army, preparing to go to the front with his horse, August 1914

A dog brings food to German troops in forward positions on the Western Front.

artillery, new weapons and other military equipment for the next assault – the list of requirements was endless. The volume of all these supplies was astronomical. In mid-1917, for example, the British army alone required 500,000 shells a day. On some days, this figure rose to one million shells a day.

All the supplies for the front were collected in huge military depots well behind the front line. They were then carried up to the line by horse or lorry, often covering the last few kilometres at night so as not to alert the enemy. Once the supplies reached the reserve trench, they then had to be carried through the communication trenches by hand to the support and frontline trenches.

One of the main problems faced by both sides was the lack of good roads. What were once small, quiet country lanes in rural France or Belgium suddenly became vital supply routes. Columns of marching men, laden horses and lorries, munitions wagons, field ambulances and other vehicles went up to the front along these roads, passing exhausted and often wounded soldiers and empty wagons coming back in the other direction. The Germans had a good network of railways to bring up men and supplies, but both sides struggled at times to keep the front adequately fed and supplied in order to maintain full battle readiness.

COMMUNICATIONS

Communicating with their front line was another problem faced by both armies, because military headquarters were often many kilometres behind the front line. The main form of communication on both sides was the field telephone, which relayed voice and Morse code messages. Teams of military engineers risked their lives to install the cables and make sure they were in working order, as enemy fire often cut the lines. If this occurred, signal grenades and rockets conveying pre-arranged messages, and flare shells carrying documents, could be used instead. Both sides also used pigeons to carry messages, but the noise of battle often confused the birds, which then flew off in the wrong direction!

HORSES AT WAR

This was also a war fought by horses, just as wars had always been fought for centuries. There was roughly one horse for every three men at war, with perhaps 20 million or more horses involved on all fronts during the four-year conflict. In 1914 the British army alone mobilised 165,000 horses, both as mounts for cavalry soldiers and as draught animals for the artillery and infantry divisions.

Horses – and donkeys – were far better at coping with muddy conditions than wheeled vehicles, but they needed large amounts of food, not all of which was readily available in a war zone. Providing supplies for the horses was a constant problem.

☛ HUMAN SUPPLIES

All armies required huge numbers of new soldiers.

Great Britain
◆ 465,712 regulars and reservists in August 1914
◆ 2,631,000 men volunteered by February 1916
◆ 2,339,000 men conscripted after February 1916

France
◆ 3,780,000 regulars and reservists in August 1914
◆ 4,707,000 men conscripted and volunteered by November 1918

Belgium
◆ 117,000 regulars and reservists in August 1914
◆ 150,000 men conscripted by November 1918

Germany
◆ 3,800,000 regulars and reservists in August 1914
◆ 7,200,000 men conscripted by November 1918

BOMBARDMENT!

When the war started in 1914, few soldiers realised that artillery would play such a major role. Most had expected to fight in open combat, but the development of the trench systems soon taught them otherwise.

USES OF ARTILLERY

Soldiers quickly learnt that full-frontal attacks on an enemy trench resulted in a high number of casualties, as the troops ran straight into a wall of enemy gunfire. New techniques and weapons were required to dislodge an enemy from its trench. Artillery could destroy a trench before an attack began. It also softened up or demoralised enemy soldiers by raining down lethal shellfire that left many injured or dead and many more stunned by the noise and ferocity of the attack. Artillery could

A British 9.2-inch howitzer in action on the Western Front.

SHELL POWER

◆ Shells are classified according to either weight or diameter and are used in both light field artillery and heavy artillery. Artillery is classified according to the size of the shell projected.

◆ Two main types of shell were used in the war. High-explosive shells, which exploded on impact with the ground, were mainly used against fortifications. Anti-personnel shrapnel shells, which exploded in flight, releasing a shower of steel balls much like a huge, airborne shotgun, were used against the trenches and against infantry fighting on open ground.

◆ Both sides used vast numbers of shells. The French army averaged 900,000 a month in 1914, rising to 4.5 million a month in 1916, while the German army averaged eight million shells a month by 1918. Before the attack on Messines Ridge on 7 June 1917, the British fired 3.5 million shells in 12 days, or three-and-a-half shells per second.

◆ In order to supply this massive demand, vast new munitions factories were set up in Britain, France and Germany to mass-produce shells. Without them, the war would have been lost.

In this cross-section, British soldiers (left) attempt to undermine a German trench; on the right German soldiers dig a countermine.

UNDERMINING THE FRONT

As well as bombarding enemy trenches from above, both sides tried to undermine them from below. Teams of military engineers and miners built tunnels under enemy trenches, which they then filled with explosives and detonated when required. Occasionally, rival teams of miners met and fought underground.

The most successful mining operation occurred under Messines Ridge near Ypres in Belgium on 7 June 1917. British engineers installed one million pounds of TNT in 21 mine chambers 20-30 metres under the ground. The resulting explosion removed large parts of the ridge and killed 10,000 or more Germans. When the charge went off it was so loud it was heard in London.

Two of the mines were not detonated, and when a later German attack overran British headquarters, their precise locations were lost. One mine exploded during a thunderstorm in 1955; the only casualty was a cow. The other is still somewhere underneath the Belgian countryside.

also be used to knock out opposing artillery positions, disrupt lines of communication, prevent reinforcements reaching the front and break up a full-frontal attack.

TWO TYPES

The types of artillery available changed considerably during the war. The two main kinds were light field guns, pulled into position on the battlefield by horses but vulnerable to machine-gun fire, and heavier guns, such as howitzers and mortars, moved by tractor onto reinforced beds behind the battlefield. Once in place, they were camouflaged. Some howitzers were so big that they were moved on railway tracks and their shells were winched inside them using a rope and tackle.

THE CREEPING BARRAGE

At first, artillery bombardments were light in firepower and short in duration. As both sides strengthened their trenches and other defensive positions, bombardments became heavier and more prolonged. But the main problem faced by both sides was that heavy artillery was often some way behind the troops, which often meant that the shells hit their own side.

As the war progressed, more accurate artillery overcame this problem. Troops could now safely advance on enemy lines behind a creeping barrage of firepower that rained down a slowly moving curtain of shells just ahead of the attacking front line. This barrage cleared both the enemy trenches and any defensive positions behind them, allowing troops to advance through enemy lines into open ground.

"... there gushed out and up enormous volumes of scarlet flame and of earth and smoke..."

Philip Gibbs, British war correspondent, on Messines Ridge, 7 June 1917

OVER THE TOP

Every soldier fighting in the trenches knew that he would be ordered to go "over the top" one day. This meant to climb out over the top of the trench parapet and advance across no-man's-land into battle with the enemy. It was the moment soldiers faced with mixed emotions.

READY FOR BATTLE?

For some, this was what they came to the Western Front for – to fight the enemy and win the war – and they approached the moment with great confidence. Others were aware that they faced death or injury, and obeyed their orders with great nervousness. Despite the hours of training, and the days and months of living in the trench, no one really knew what to expect when the order to advance was given. As the hour approached, excitement, anticipation, fear and sometimes sheer terror spread along the trench.

In the days leading up to the attack, the enemy positions were bombarded to soften them up or hopefully wipe them out altogether. In theory, a bombardment that was well aimed could smash up the barbed-wire defences, leaving the ground clear for an all-out assault. In practice, however, this rarely happened, as bombardments were not that complete or effective. Gun emplacements were difficult to knock out, and any gaps created in the defence could always be filled quickly by highly mobile machine-gunners. Against them, troops laden with heavy equipment and armed only with a rifle and bayonet, advancing slowly over muddy, broken ground stood little chance.

FIRST DAY ON THE SOMME

The principle of bombarding the enemy into submission before an infantry attack was tried disastrously at the Battle of the Somme. On 24 June 1916 a massive British artillery bombardment began that continued for six days. The British fired more than two million shells, but did not concentrate their fire on German weak spots and failed to destroy dug-outs and gun emplacements.

On 1 July at 7.30 am, the barrage stopped and the British troops slowly advanced across no-man's-land, where they were machine-gunned by German soldiers emerging from the safety of their deep trenches. On the first day alone, 57,470 men were killed or injured, two for every metre of the 28-kilometre front. In the entire 142-day battle, 1.2 million men on both sides were killed or wounded. It was the bloodiest battle in human history.

Soldiers on all sides carried bayonets that slotted onto the ends of their rifles for close-quarter fighting. This is a German Mauser bayonet.

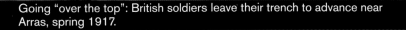

Going "over the top": British soldiers leave their trench to advance near Arras, spring 1917.

THE DEATH TOLL

This uneven battle between advancing troops and a dug-in enemy explains some of the massive losses on the Western Front. On the first day of the Battle of the Somme – 1 July 1916 – one British corporal reported: "We never got near the Germans. Our lads were mown down. You couldn't do anything. The machine-guns were levelled and they were mowing the top of the trenches. … It was hopeless. And those young officers, going ahead, they were picked off like flies."

Sometimes the carnage was so great that the defenders refused to continue firing. At the Battle of Loos in September 1915, the British advanced to within 90 metres of the German line before their machine-gunners opened fire. "Suddenly all hell was let loose", reported a British soldier. "Some men began to stumble and fall, machine-guns were firing from the front of us. … I'll remember the sight to my dying day, the whole slope was full of prone figures. The Germans suddenly stopped firing … they were so full of bitter remorse and guilt at the corpses that they refused to fire another shot", allowing the injured to stagger back across no-man's-land.

☛ **REFUSAL TO FIGHT**

◆ Not every soldier obeyed orders and went into battle. Some ran away (technically, an act of desertion), while others refused to fight or were too terrified to move.

◆ Most men who would not fight were not cowards. They were more frightened by fear itself than by death, something most troops felt.

◆ In order to keep discipline, armies tried deserters, usually for "cowardice in the face of the enemy", and if found guilty, shot them. To spare their feelings, next-of-kin were usually told that they had been killed in action.

◆ 346 British soldiers were shot for desertion, refusing to obey orders, cowardice or for criminal acts.

◆ In the French army, the number of deserters rose from 509 in 1914 to 21,174 in 1917. Most of these were individual acts, apart from a mass mutiny in spring 1917, when an enormous attack against German positions led to 130,000 casualties and few gains. Some soldiers refused to fight.

By the end of June 1917 almost half the French army reported acts of mutiny. The new commander-in-chief, General Pétain, averted a total mutiny by restoring morale. However, many thousands were arrested, 3,427 were found guilty and 554 condemned to death.

CARING FOR THE INJURED

It was a vast operation to care for the injured on the Western Front. Some soldiers were patched up and sent back into battle, while others had to be sent home for a long, perhaps permanent, period of recovery.

RECOVERING THE INJURED AND DEAD

The most gruesome task undertaken on the front was recovering the injured and the dead from the battlefield and from no-man's-land. Some were horribly wounded or mutilated, others had been killed on the barbed-wire fences or had lain dead for days. Stretcher parties of volunteers, soldiers and prisoners of war undertook this appalling job, often under enemy fire.

MASSIVE INJURIES

The range of injuries to be treated was immense. Most were wounds caused by flying shrapnel from shells or through bullets, but those soldiers unlucky enough to be caught at the receiving end of an artillery barrage suffered terrible injuries and even suffocation if buried alive under tonnes of earth and wooden props. Injuries to bones could be healed, but facial injuries were far more difficult to treat, as were the terrible effects of gas (see pages 24-25). Trench living itself generated many illnesses, as the unsanitary conditions bred cholera, dysentery, tetanus and typhoid. Infectious diseases, such as measles and meningitis, were inevitable with so many men living together in such close quarters. In the last year of the war, many soldiers also fell victim to the worldwide influenza epidemic, which killed more than were lost in battle that year.

RECEIVING CARE

An injured soldier was first taken to the regimental aid post off one of the second-line support trenches. If the injury required more attention, the soldier was then carried or taken by stretcher back to the casualty

"We set to work to bury people. We pushed them into the sides of trenches but bits of them kept getting uncovered and sticking out, like people in a badly made bed ... The bottom of the trench was springy like a mattress because of all the bodies underneath ..."

Leonard Thompson, quoted in *Akenfield* by Ronald Blythe

clearing station about 10 kilometres behind the front. These were mostly farmhouses, factories, churches or war-damaged buildings taken over for the war effort. Here the wounded received proper treatment and even basic surgery from professional and volunteer nurses. Care was basic, however, and the wounded were often left to look after themselves and each other.

If the clearing station could not cope, the wounded were taken by ambulance to a military hospital well back from the front. The aim was to return the soldier to active duty as soon as possible. If that was not practical, the injured soldier was invalided home to a convalescent hospital. For the British, this meant leaving France and returning home to "Blighty". After a long period in the trenches, a "Blighty wound" which sent them home, providing it was not too serious and not in the wrong place, came as a blessed relief.

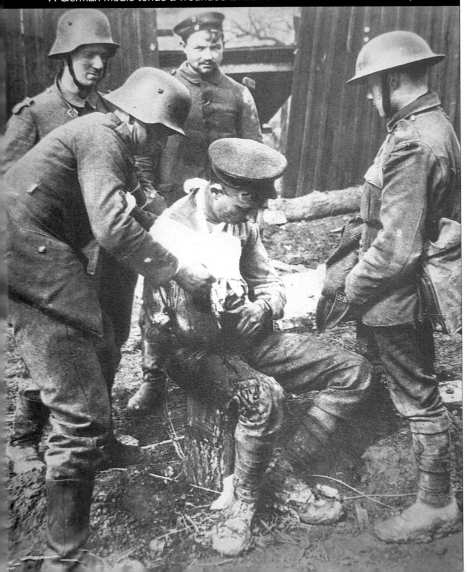

A German medic tends a wounded British soldier on the Western Front, 1917.

SHELLSHOCK

During the war, a new illness appeared and was given the name shellshock. Its symptoms were severe – nightmares, flashbacks, uncontrolled weeping and guilt at having survived when other soldiers had died – but many people doubted that it really existed. Most thought that it was a personality defect such as cowardice or loss of nerve in the face of battle. They claimed that if the patient only "got a grip on himself" or "pulled himself together" it would disappear.

Today, shellshock is known as post-traumatic stress disorder (PTSD) and is properly recognised as a serious illness. Faced with a life in which there is no meaning – where the killing and horror of war have no purpose at all – a patient suffers a complete emotional and psychological collapse. Today, it is recognised that many of those 346 British soldiers shot for cowardice, desertion and other reasons, probably suffered from PTSD. They were ill – not cowardly.

GAS ATTACK

The war saw the introduction of a number of new and terrifying weapons. None was more frightening than toxic gas, which poisoned and often killed its victims within minutes.

THE FIRST ATTACKS

The first time gas was used during the war was in August 1914, when French troops used tear-gas grenades against advancing Germans. However, the first large-scale use of gas was by German forces on the Eastern Front at Bolimov, in what is now Poland, on 31 January 1915. Here German artillery bombarded

Blinded by a gas attack, British soldiers rely on each other for guidance as they queue up for treatment in 1917.

the Russian lines with 18,000 shells of xylyl bromide, a type of tear gas, but the liquid gas largely failed to evaporate in the intense cold.

Gas was first used on the Western Front on 22 April 1915, during the Second Battle of Ypres. French-Algerian troops noticed a greenish-yellow cloud moving towards them from the German lines. They panicked as it reached them because they had no protection against the deadly chlorine. From then on, both sides used gas – the Germans about 68,000 tonnes, the French almost 37,000 tonnes, and the British, who first used it at the Battle of Loos in 1915, more than 25,000 tonnes.

"The chaps were all gasping and couldn't breathe, and it was ghastly, especially for the chaps that were wounded. The gasping, the gasping!"

Sergeant Bill Hay describes a gas attack at Ypres, 26 April 1915

LETHAL EFFECTS

The first effects of gas were felt on the face and in the eyes, but within seconds it entered the nose and throat, causing coughing and choking. The long-term effects depended on the type of gas used. Some killed quickly, some resulted in blindness or skin blisters, while others caused the lungs to collapse and fill with liquid. In total, some 1,200,000 soldiers on both sides were gassed, of whom at least 90,000 died.

PROTECT AND SURVIVE

Troops had to wear protective clothing and even horses were provided with simple respirators. At first this was simply a pair of goggles and a fabric mouth-pad. By 1916 troops wore protective helmets, fully covering the face and protecting the eyes, nose and throat. A filter inside the attached respirator neutralised the gas, allowing the soldier to breathe. It saved lives but was uncomfortable and hot to wear and restricted vision and movement at a time when both were essential.

☞ GAS FACTS

- ◆ The first gas vapour clouds were released from canisters and blown with the wind towards enemy lines, but these caused chaos if the wind changed direction or failed to blow.
- ◆ Gas shells, which were fired at enemy lines, were more effective. These contained liquid gas, which evaporated on impact. Many types of gas were used, with different results.
- ◆ Chlorine, diphosgene and phosgene caused intense breathing difficulties. Benzyl caused the eyes to water. Dichlorethylsulphide, known as mustard gas because of its smell, burnt the skin and caused temporary blindness. Eventually it flooded the lungs, leading to death from suffocation.
- ◆ Mustard gas was feared the most, as it attacked the skin through normal clothing. Protective body suits were not available during the war.

LEFT OVER FROM THE WAR

Even today, more than 80 years after the end of the war, unexploded gas and artillery shells, grenades and other armaments are still being uncovered along what used to be the Western Front. In the Belgian village of Boesinghe, near Ypres, work on a new industrial estate was halted in 2001 when an entire buried trench system was unearthed, containing a large number of unexploded gas shells. Each spring, Belgian farmers plough up shells and grenades that might still be live. As a result of this, Belgium has one of the busiest army bomb disposal units in the world.

WRITING IN WARTIME

With long hours of inaction in the trenches, many soldiers filled their time by writing letters home. Others produced poetry, some of which was the most remarkable verse of the 20th century.

WRITING HOME

Many soldiers had never been away from home before and they wrote regular letters, often for the first time in their lives. These letters were vetted and sometimes censored by the military authorities in case they revealed secrets of use to the enemy. The censors removed anything that might undermine civilian morale, for the true horrors of the trenches were not common knowledge at home. Many soldiers also kept diaries, which proved useful for war historians to read.

Soldiers also set up their own newspapers, the most famous of which was the British-run *Wipers Times*, named after the common English pronunciation of the Belgian city of Ypres. Some also formed drama groups, while many read books as never before.

LITERATURE

The main literature to emerge from the war was poetry. Until 1914 most war poetry was concerned with honour and was very patriotic. But during the war, new young poets emerged who had fought in the trenches. They

THE WAR ARTISTS

Many soldiers took their paintbrushes with them to the front, and recorded some of the events they witnessed. Others took up drawing and illustrated their letters home with sketches of trenches and fellow soldiers. Governments, however, wanted an official record of the war, as well as propaganda material, and commissioned artists to visit the front.

The first British war artists, such as Paul Nash and CRW Nevinson, were commissioned in 1916, while the French sent artists to specific parts of the front in early 1917. British and French artists were also employed in special camouflage units. The British painter Norman Wilkinson designed the dazzle camouflage that confused the outlines of ships and made it difficult for German U-boats to attack them accurately.

"In Flanders fields the poppies blow
Between the crosses, row on row,
That mark our place; and in the sky,
The larks, still bravely singing, fly
Scarce heard amid the guns below."

From "In Flanders Fields", by John McCrae, Canadian war poet

Allied soldiers in World War One posted home embroidered souvenirs such as these to their loved ones.

wrote at first in sadness and then in outrage. When Wilfred Owen, a British soldier and poet, wrote that "My subject is War, and the pity of War", he approached his subject in a way that no poet before him had ever done.

Much of this war poetry is very intense and personal. It is also very sad, as many of the poets themselves died in the trenches. The work of these poets is now considered among the finest literature of the past century, read by many for contemplation and study. Every November, on Remembrance Day, the words of one of these poets – Laurence Binyon, who wrote "For The Fallen" in September 1914 – are read out to recall the dead of both world wars:

"They shall not grow old, as we that are left grow old;
Age shall not weary them, nor the years condemn.
At the going down of the sun and in the morning
We will remember them."

THE LOST GENERATION

Many published poets died during the war, either in battle or as a result of illness. Among the most famous were:

Guillaume Apollinaire (French): Died of influenza, two days before the armistice in November 1918

Rupert Brooke (British): Died of blood poisoning in Greece, 1915

Francis Ledwidge (Irish): Hit by a stray shell in Flanders, 1917

John McCrae (Canadian): Died of pneumonia in France, 1918

Wilfred Owen (British): Killed in France on 4 November 1918, one week before the armistice

Charles Péguy (French): Shot while observing a German retreat in France, September 1914

Isaac Rosenberg (British): Killed in France, 1918

THE END OF THE TRENCHES

In spring 1918, the fourth year of the war, there appeared to be no end in sight to the stalemate on the Western Front. The trenches threatened to become permanent. Yet six months later the war was over and the trenches were soon filled in.

WEAKENING GERMANY

The main reason for this sudden change was that the advantage tipped decisively in favour of the Allies. By early 1918 Germany was becoming increasingly weakened by the Allied naval blockade that prevented desperately needed war materials reaching its factories. Its allies – Austria-Hungary, the Ottoman Empire and Bulgaria – were on the point of collapse.

In March 1918, however, Germany signed a peace treaty with Russia, its main enemy in the east, and began to move all its troops on to the Western Front. There, however, they would soon meet the million fresh troops on their way from the USA. Germany therefore decided to deliver a knockout blow against the Allies before the US troops were ready. The attack began in March 1918 and saw the Germans make considerable gains. But their supplies ran low and their troops became tired. On 18 July the attack ground to a halt. The German army had over-reached its capabilities.

THE DECISIVE BLOW

The Allies seized the opportunity. On 8 August 456 British tanks rolled forwards near Amiens, supported by largely Canadian and Australian infantry and a highly accurate, rolling artillery barrage that, this time, destroyed all before it. Along almost the entire Western Front, the Allies enjoyed an overwhelming military and technological superiority in tanks, aircraft and artillery, as well as men, and surged ahead.

As the Allies pushed forwards, their tanks proved to be the decisive factor. On 29 September the British

THE AMERICANS ARRIVE

On 2 April 1917, US President Woodrow Wilson asked Congress to declare war on Germany to make the world "safe for democracy". Its army, however was small – 128,000 men, with a further 131,500 men in the National Guard. It had few munitions, no large guns and only 55 aircraft. By June 1917, 9.6 million men had registered for national service and started training. Not long after, the first expeditionary force of 14,000 men arrived in France.

At first the US troops were poorly trained and ill prepared for the Western Front, but from April 1918, 300,000 highly trained and well equipped troops began to arrive in Europe every month. Their contribution was to prove decisive.

All combatants in World War One issued medals to their soldiers. On the left is the German Iron Cross awarded for bravery; on the right the British War Medal, handed out to all British and British Empire citizens who participated in the war.

broke through the supposedly impregnable defences of the German Hindenburg line and emerged into open country. As a South African major serving with the British army remarked: "From then onward the evil of the old trench warfare was a thing of the past."

The trenches lasted as long as they did because neither side had the technological superiority to overcome them. When that situation changed in autumn 1918, the defensive trenches became irrelevant. The Allies had learnt how to co-ordinate men, artillery, tanks, planes and supplies into one unified force and take the offensive. With that mighty force, they were able to smash the German trenches and, on 11 November 1918, bring the war to an end.

The End Of The War

30 September German government resigns after defeats on the Western Front.

4 October Prince Max von Baden becomes German chancellor and appeals for an armistice, accepting Wilson's "Fourteen Points" for peace.

27 October General Ludendorff, German commander on the Western Front, resigns as the Allies overwhelm his armies.

3 November German fleet mutinies at Kiel and discontent spreads throughout Germany.

7 November German armistice commission led by Matthias Erzberger asks for a meeting with General Foch, supreme Allied commander. The commission travels overnight through enemy lines and begins discussions with Foch in his railway carriage in the forest of Compiègne in eastern France.

9 November Kaiser Wilhelm II abdicates and flees to Holland; Germany becomes a republic.

5 am, 11 November Erzberger signs an armistice with the Allies.

11 am, 11 November The armistice comes into effect; the war is over.

"11 o'clock came, and a sudden silence! It was impossible to realise that the war was over ... it was no longer necessary to wear our steel hats or gas masks!"

Lieutenant Ruffell,
British soldier, November 1918

GLOSSARY

Alliance A formal agreement or pact, often military, between two or more nations.

Allies, the Britain, France, Russia and the other nations, including the USA, who fought on the same side in World War One.

Armistice An agreement between opposing sides to cease fire while a peace settlement is agreed; the armistice that was signed between Germany and the Allies to end the war came into effect at 11 am on 11 November 1918.

Artillery Light field guns and heavier guns, such as mortars, howitzers and so on, used to attack an enemy line.

Blighty British soldiers' slang term for home.

Cavalry Soldiers who fight on horseback.

Central Powers Germany, Austria-Hungary and later the Ottoman Empire and Bulgaria, who fought as allies in World War One.

Conscript A person who is enrolled compulsorily for military service.

Division A major formation of troops; in the British army, a division consisted of three brigades, or about 20,000 men.

Empire A large area of land made up of different countries and peoples, ruled by one nation and its emperor.

Flanders Low-lying border country between France and Belgium.

Flank The exposed side of an army formation as it marches forwards.

Front The area where two opposing armies face each other, also known as the front line.

Hun British slang term for a German.

Infantry Soldiers who fight on foot.

Machine-gun A rapid-firing automatic gun, usually mounted on a tripod, capable of firing up to 600 bullets a minute.

Militia A local military force of volunteer citizens.

Mobilise To prepare an army for war; a general mobilisation includes all the armed services and many civilian services.

Mutiny An open rebellion by soldiers or seamen against their officers, usually punishable by death.

Neutral A nation that refuses to take sides in a war and does not fight.

Recruit A person who joins an army voluntarily.

Shrapnel Pellets, bullets or other small pieces of metal thrown out of a shell after it explodes.

Volunteer *see* **Recruit**

INDEX

A

Allies 6-8, 12, 28, 29, 30
ammunition 11, 13, 16
armies, size of 8-9, 17
armistice 27, 29, 30
artillery 14, 17, 18-19, 20, 22, 24, 25, 28-30

B

Battle of the Somme 20-21
Binyon, Laurence 27

C

casualties 11, 18, 20-23, 25
Central Powers 6, 28, 30
communications 17, 19
communication trench 10, 11, 17
conscript 8, 9, 17, 30

D

desertion 21, 23

E

Expeditionary Force 7, 8, 9, 10

F

Foch, General 29
front line 10, 11, 13, 14, 16, 17, 19, 22, 23, 30

G

gas attack 22, 24-25
guns 11, 12, 13, 16, 17, 18, 19, 20, 28, 30

H

headquarters 11, 17, 19
horses 16, 17, 19, 25
hospital 23

I

illness 12, 22, 27
injured, the 12, 13, 17, 20-23, 24, 25
intelligence gathering 14-15

K

kit 12, 13, 16
Kitchener, Lord 8, 9

L

letter-writing 12, 26
literature 26-27

M

machine-gun 11, 19, 20, 21, 31
Messines Ridge 18, 19
military service 6, 8, 9
munitions 17, 18, 28

N

no-man's-land 10-15, 20-22

O

Owen, Wilfred 27

P

Pétain, General 21
poetry-writing 26-27

R

rations 13, 16
refusal to fight 21
Remembrance Day 27
reserve trench 10, 11, 13, 17
reservist 9, 17

S

shells 11, 14, 15, 17, 18, 19, 20, 22, 25, 27, 31
shellshock 23
supplies 11, 12, 16-17, 28, 29
support trench 10, 11, 22

T

trench,
    design 10-11
    everyday life in 11, 12-13, 26

U

undermining 19

V

volunteer 6, 8, 9, 17, 22, 31

W

war artists 26
war writing 12, 26
weapon 17, 24
Western Front 6-7, 8, 10, 13-16, 18, 20-23, 25, 28, 29
Wilson, President Woodrow 28, 29